# Just Do it:
# Rules to go from the School Run to the Boardroom

Written by
**Laura Rigney**

Published by
**Negotiis Books**

ISBN-13: 978-1502820778

# Introduction

**W**hen you hear the word mumpreneur what's the first image that pops into your mind? Everybody sees something different but for me it was an idyllic scene. A mother, having started an instantly successful internet company, sitting in her perfectly manicured country garden working from her laptop whilst her young children play happily with the family dog. Everybody is happy, calm and serene. When lunchtime comes around, mother instantly whips up a healthy, nutritious lunch that the children are delighted with and eat without argument. Of course, the mother sits with the children to eat lunch and they have a little chat about what games to play after eating. After lunch they all partake in a fun yet educational game and have quality time until supper beckons. Yet again another, almost magically perfect meal is put together with no fuss and it's on the table just in time for father to walk through the door, admire his immaculate home and greet his perfect family blah, blah, blah.

The fact of the matter is, that unless you are a super hero with the ultimate mixture of Supernanny's child rearing skills, Fanny Craddocks meal creation capabilities, a fetish for Mr Muscle products and have the business acumen of Lord Alan Sugar, it's not that easy. Life as a mumpreneur can be one of the most rewarding experiences imaginable but let's be honest, it's tough. Waking at ridiculous hours of the morning to get emails sent before the children wake, taking part in conference calls whilst making breakfast and trying to get to and from meetings in between school run times can drive a woman insane.

You may read this and think why on earth I do it if it's so tough? The honest truth is that it's an amazing experience. The creation of a company from a seed of an idea, watching your business grow and become part of your everyday life and at the same time being able to raise your children, go to nativity plays and be the one that puts them to bed every night is a dream imagined by thousands of women every day, and a reality for thousands of others.

Let me give you a little background information. I had worked in sales since leaving school and when pregnant with my first baby I thought it would be the perfect opportunity to start some kind of business. Fate apparently had other plans for me and after four months of maternity leave I was asked to return to work. Fast forward two years and I was pregnant with my second child. This time I looked into the idea a little more seriously and even planned to start a business with my sister. Once baby number two had been born I realised that trying to start a business with two pre-school children was something I could never do. A hop, skip and jump four months down the line and I was once again with child. I was shocked but never the less delighted with our situation and promptly explained to my boss that the likelihood of me returning to work was slim. She then offered me the perfect solution, or so it seemed at the time. I was given the opportunity to work self-employed from home doing the same job I had always done but without having to worry about childcare. Perfect. Or so I thought.

Once baby number two was welcomed into the world, I was itching to do something that didn't involve, breast pads, nappies or baby grows and started working for my employer on a self-employed basis. In theory, this should have suited me and my family perfectly but my job at the time was telesales. I had to convince businesses to buy advertising in directories, a job I'd always done extremely well in, until halfway through my pitch for a  potential £4500.00 sale, I suddenly heard my little ones in the background. The man I was trying to sell to was a 50 something CEO and thought my circumstances were highly unprofessional. He immediately told me exactly what he thought (which wasn't at all pleasant) and hung up. I realised that this way of working was unrealistic, how was I supposed to sell anything to anyone with babies crying and toddlers asking for juice at the same time? Giving in doesn't come naturally to me but I decided for the good of my sanity and my children to give up working completely and become a fully-fledged housewife.

I'm sure you're wondering why I'm telling you my little sob story. If this sequence of events hadn't taken place then I wouldn't be running my own business whilst being a partner in another. I wouldn't even be writing this book. Most women at some time or another consider starting their own business and many do so very successfully. I'm willing to bet that nearly every employed, pregnant woman seriously considered starting a business whilst on maternity leave but I happen to know that very few do anything more than think about it, until recently that is. In the last few years there has been a huge surge in the number of mothers starting a business at the same time as being a full time parent.

# Rule One: It's not a hobby

The biggest problem we face as a business sector is the fact that we're not taken seriously. It all goes back to the fact that mum-preneurs or table top tycoons as we were previously known were all considered to be bored, full time housewives and mothers who took up hobbies to fill their time. Now, first things first, as anyone who is a full time mother would know, after having your first child you would do anything to have any spare time whatsoever. Once your baby is delivered into the family home your days are filled with feeding, nappy changing, washing cleaning, cooking and that's if you're lucky enough to have a contented child, so the thought that we all sit around drinking cups of tea and watching daytime TV is something I frankly find hilarious.

Even after being in business for four years my friends and family still don't really see it as anything other than a glorified hobby. The perfect example of this is my father (who I love dearly just in case you get the wrong idea.). I'm lucky enough to be able to work from my laptop on the go so I regularly go and spend the day with my folks and work from their kitchen table. As soon as I sit down and get the laptop up and running my Dad asks what I'm doing. When I explain that I'm working his response is always the same, 'Working?! Doing what exactly?' Regardless of the fact that I have built a successful company and I'm a partner in the UKs leading support organisations for mumpreneurs, my dear old Dad can't seem to comprehend that I DO work. In fact, mumpreneurs probably work longer hours than most other sectors because of the time restrictions we're presented with.

When you make the decision to set out on your own you need to ensure that you are taken seriously as a business woman. Now I don't want to encourage deceitfulness but if I had my time again I wouldn't have told a living soul what I was doing. I would have researched my market whilst the kids were napping and my husband was at work. I would have written my business plan in the dead of night when nobody was around to question me or my motivation and I certainly wouldn't have run around telling everyone about my great idea and the fact that I, yes little old me, intended to start a business whilst looking after three small children.

I would have planned absolutely everything and once typed up into an official business plan I would have made several copies that I could hand out whenever anybody made a sly remark, gave me a sarcastic glance or provided me with one of those 'let's just humour her' smiles.

I'm not trying to put you off starting up but you need to be taken seriously by those around you. Your family and friends will become your support network and if they don't believe in you, you'll soon start doubting yourself. Luckily, I'm fairly thick skinned and I know my Dad doesn't mean any harm, he's just an old fashioned Irish man who worries profusely and wants the best for me.

Once you have your business plan finalised, sit and read through it using your critical head. You need to view it the way others will. Think about the kind of questions your nearest and dearest will ask you and try to have answers prepared. Make sure that, when questioned, you answer in a business-like fashion even if you're talking to your oldest and closest friend of twenty years, your attitude towards your business will go a long way towards increasing others belief and confidence in you.

The biggest thing to remember though is to have faith in yourself and your idea. You can start your own business, anyone can, and you can make a success of it if you have the right amount of dedication and determination. Your new mantra should now be, 'I AM a serious business woman and can achieve anything I put my mind to'. Now repeat five times each day to prevent doubt creeping in.

# Rule two: Finding your confidence

This goes hand in hand with rule one. Regardless of how anyone else perceives you, you need to have the confidence to go through with it.

Confidence is a tricky thing. One day you think you're overflowing with the stuff and feel like you can take on the world but the next you start to doubt whether or not this whole business idea was ever viable. I know I wasn't alone in spending many an hour and multiple sleepless nights wondering why I was even bothering and then considering the back-to-work options. I'm pretty sure there's a little fella in the back of our minds who just sits and waits for the tiniest shred of doubt to appear. Once he sees it coming his way he jumps, grabbing on to it with both hands and begins planting little pieces of it all over our brains. The trick here is to give him a good talking to and if that doesn't work, an extremely vigorous kicking should do the trick.

In my humble opinion, lack of confidence in women really begins to develop after the birth of their first baby. Think about it. You're the centre of attention for nine whole months with everyone telling you how great you look, how you're glowing and how you're going to make a fabulous mother then D day arrives. Once you've given birth to your little bundle of joy, very few people even ask how you are. The constant stream of visiting relatives not only brings beautiful little gifts for the new-born, they also bring titbits of what they consider to be helpful parenting advice.

The fact that you've read every parenting book published since the turn of the century, and feel completely ready to be a mother hasn't occurred to any of your well-wishers who keep spouting out unneeded and unrequested advice. Then after the first two or three days the visitors stop coming and you're left alone with a helpless, defenceless little baby and the minute you question yourself that little fella pops up and helps spread your self-doubt until you feel useless. In the space of weeks you've gone from feeling like a confident, competent mother to an uneducated, blubbering mess and that's if you're lucky enough not to have the added pressure of post natal depression.

The reality is that you are able to cope. Most of these advice givers are only trying to help,, and they don't realise that in doing so they are probably making you feel like a spec of inadequate dust floating around your own home. This feeling never really leaves you and when you start a business it's not uncommon for all of those insecurities and feelings of self-doubt to come flooding back into the forefront of your mind. Just remember that they aren't your doubts, they are the doubts of other people that have been passed onto you.

One of the most common confidence issues I hear is mumpreneurs being unable to chat on the phone to other business owners and this becomes an even bigger problem when the time comes that they need to speak to CEO's and MD's of larger corporations. The fact of the matter is that even these individuals who have climbed the corporate ladder or scaled the self-employment mountain to become who they are, were once in the same position as you are now. At some point they were the office junior, the tea boy or the nervous person at the end of the phone registering as self-employed for the first time.

Instead of being intimidated by these people, be inspired by them. Use them as your motivation. If they have done it, why can't you? If all else fails and you still feel unable to deal with these calls, use that age old trick of picturing them naked; just don't let it distract you from the task at hand.

# Rule Three: Your to-do list is king

You need to be organised. Fact. You will be running a business, looking after children, doing the school run and more than likely, still be the one in charge of keeping the house in order.

It's a little hypocritical of me to be telling you about organisation. If you could see my office you would understand why. When I worked for my previous employer, I was the most organised person in the office. I had 26 business directories on my desk in magazine files sorted alphabetically. I spent half an hour at the end of every day finishing of paperwork and preparing my workload for first thing the following morning. If anybody in the office needed anything, they came to me. My, how things have changed. I suppose because I'm the only person who sees my office I'm not that fussed on keeping it in any kind of order, the problem however is that because my office is in my spare bedroom, my household paperwork is no longer organised either. Everything is in one big pile to be filed, a pile that I started almost a year ago.

Up until recently, I would go to bed and create a list in my mind of all the jobs I had to complete the following day. Great in theory, not that great in practice. Since starting my business my memory has gone from being great to being non-existent. Therefore, every morning when I wake up, I have no recollection of the endless list of tasks that my brain had stored the night before. I swear, somewhere in my head is a filing cabinet overflowing with incomplete tasks and at some point It'll explode and I'll probably have a breakdown!

Now I keep a pad and pen at the side of my bed so that I can keep a physical list of things that require attention. It's a must to do this. You can guarantee that the minute you lay your head on that fluffy pillow and start drifting into much needed sleep that something requiring urgent attention pops into your head. Write it down! Don't be fooled into thinking that this list will be kept exclusively for work related tasks, you will soon find that you start adding own clothes day for school, PTFA meetings and even shopping lists, but that's fine. Your private life and work life will merge into one, that's the beauty of being am mumpreneur, and you need to try and run both sides as efficiently as possible. To-Do lists will become your saving grace and will, more than likely, save you a lot of time chasing your tail.

What I now do is split my list into two parts, 'to-do' and 'urgent'. This is a great idea as rather than working through your list you will deal with the high priority items first before you start getting shouty emails that will upset the rest of your day.

I can honestly say, there are very few moments in each day that give me greater satisfaction than putting a cross through an item on my list. Sometimes I even add things to the list (if I forget to put them on in the first place) after I've completed them just so I can cross them off. It may sound like the actions of someone who needs professional help but it really is a great motivator to carry on ploughing through your jobs.

When you're preparing to start your business there should be three things at the top of your list:

- Write your business plan
- Register as self-employed with HMRC
- Set-up a direct debit to pay both NI contributions and TAX.

You may not need to pay tax in your first year; obviously it all depends on your profit levels and if you don't you will get a rebate which is always a lovely bonus. If you find you do have a tax bill after you've submitted your self-assessment, it's a very reassuring feeling knowing that your direct debits have either significantly reduced the bill or paid it all together!

# Rule Four: Getting online

Mumpreneurs are dependent on the internet. As a rule we work from home enabling us to look after our little ones at the same time so the internet is usually our only way of trading. Not only is the internet the perfect trading platform but it's also the perfect networking tool (more on that later).

In this day of laptops, iPods, iPads and numerous other technological advances that I know very little about, getting online has never been easier so you need to ensure your business has a presence on the World Wide Web. The latest statistics show that 38% of the buying public now make online purchases. In fact, the average high street store now completes 24% of its transactions online so being visible to the internet surfing public is vital. When I first realised that I needed a website I seriously panicked as it instantly set the alarm bells ringing. I was under the impression that websites required thousands of pounds of investment and as I had a start-up budget of approximately zero my initial thought was game over. I knew a few people who had built their own sites and decided to look a little further into it. Whilst my brain began trying to process random technical terms and HTML codes I came across a site that provided 'out of the box' websites. Essentially it meant that the website was already built, you simply add text, images and anything else you want to incorporate and away you go. Excited at the prospect of having my own website that I'd had a hand in creating I swiftly and unrepentantly paid a year's fee and started filling it with details of my little enterprise. I soon discovered that any fool can do this but it takes a special kind of fool to make it look anywhere near decent. Luckily, I had recently made friends with a very talented, self-taught graphic designer who helped me out a little. This very talented lady also knew all about HTML (website codes and such) and taught me a lot about them too.

My out of the box website lasted about as long as my first business which wasn't long at all but it did serve me well during the time. Since then I have discovered lots of companies that offer the same service only better. This can be the perfect solution to your initial online trading issues. Most of these companies include hosting, and prices start from as little as £2.99 per month. It's also a great way to get a feel for the demand of your service or product. Nothing speaks the truth more than sales so if you have little in the way of a start-up budget, it's a great way to get going.

As your business grows you may find that you are in need of a more bespoke web solution. If this is the case then firstly, congratulations! If your website is growing it means your business is growing too so you're doing something right! Again, the thought of a bespoke website conjures up images of pound signs but if you find the right developer and designer it's well worth the financial outlay. You can probably expect to pay anything from £599 for a bespoke website with CMS (Content Management System).

# Rule Five: Housework? What housework?

I remember a time when my house was immaculate. I have fond memories of a time when there was never a dirty dish to be seen, the ironing was always done and I struggled to get enough clothes to make a full load of washing. I recall the times when I would follow the children around tidying up their toys and always have dinner cooking when my husband came home from work. Those days are long gone. Imagine a 1950s housewife and you have a vague image of me during my first months as a stay at home mum.

It's so easy to imagine yourself as superwoman. Business woman/mother by day, super cleaner by night. Don't kid yourself. You need to be fully prepared for what awaits you. I work all day every day, by the time I've finished I'm too exhausted to clean so it builds up and builds up. Every Sunday I give my house a thorough clean and by Monday morning my three boys ensure it looks like a squat. I'm exaggerating a little but where cleaning used to be right up at the top of my priority list it's now slipped way, way down, so far down I can barely see it anymore. It's not unusual to find breakfast dishes on the table at lunchtime, to find dishes stacked on the draining board or to see me discreetly sneaking black bags of clean, unironed clothes into the boot of a local lady's car that I pay to iron on my behalf.

The way I see it is, I don't get paid for cleaning, washing or ironing, I get paid for working and the more I work the more I earn. The knock on effect is that I have a constant guilty feeling for the state of my house. Don't get me wrong, I'm lucky enough to have a husband who helps out, but he works long hours and is exhausted by the time he gets home from work. He's also self-employed so his earnings are directly connected to the amount of work he completes too.

After you have a baby everyone says, "don't worry about the housework, it'll still be there tomorrow". They fail to tell you that if you don't try to do it every day, it builds up and up until you start inventing excuses not to do it rather than trying to figure out where exactly to start. When you start a business it takes over your life. It's so addictive that you spend all of your spare time at your laptop, on the phone or checking emails on your Smartphone. Cleaning becomes one of those tasks that you dread, not because it's boring but because it takes you away from working.

So here are a few tips:

- Try to break the housework down into manageable tasks rather than one huge job.
- Load the washing machine whilst you're on a conference call (who will know?).
- If your children are old enough, get them to help (it's not slave labour it's character building).
- Prioritise the important jobs as you do with work.
- Make a list of jobs that need to be done every day and don't start work until they're done.
- Sometimes work takes over and you don't get things done. Don't panic it's not the end of the world.

# Rule Six: Managing your time (or lack of)

Take five minutes to sit and plan your average day once your business is up and running. Once you work out how much time you can dedicate to your business each day, half it. This will give you a more realistic idea of the amount of 'work time' you have.

Don't be alarmed if it doesn't seem much. Children are unpredictable and often need more time than you have to give. It's very demotivating to allocate three hours to your business during the day only to find that you've only managed two. The more realistic you are with your estimates the better. Remember, if you have time left over you can always get ahead of yourself. In the early days I found it easier to try and work during the evenings. Most babies settle better at that time and therefore it gives you more of an opportunity to really knuckle down and concentrate on the tasks at hand.

The reality of the situation is that those first few years with your little one are precious and you don't want to look back and regret not spending enough time with your baby. However, those are the years to start building your business and your reputation. Until your child is at least two years old you will more than likely have them with you full time which does restrict your working hours. Once they reach two it's recommended that they are placed in some kind of playgroup to help with social interaction. All of my children started playgroup aged two, for three mornings each week. The average playgroup session lasts for two and a half hours. That's seven and a half additional hours each week that you can focus on your enterprise. Once they reach pre-school that increases to twelve and a half hours each week!

Research shows that women who start businesses whilst pregnant or on maternity leave use the four years before their child starts school to research, plan and begin building their business. The company then grows slowly but steadily until the child has gone into full time education at which point the mum in question has built up the reputation, contacts and more importantly the confidence to really expand and grow the business. This slow but steady approach is what gives us the edge over men. I'm not about to get into a men vs women debate but it is proven that women take less risks in business and my belief is that this is because they take things so much slower. This does of course mean that it takes longer for you to begin reaping the rewards of your hard work but it also means that there's a stronger chance that your business will go the distance.

Remember the fable of the tortoise and the hare? You're the tortoise. Slow and steady wins the race!

# Rule Seven: Joining the circus

Women are famous for having the ability to multi-task effortlessly. Unless of course, you're me. I'm useless at it and I envy those women who use one arm to feed the baby and another to send an email. For me it's like trying to read Greek, impossible. But for the majority of women, multi-tasking is second nature. This is a great skill to have as you'll be using it every single day.

Now I know I said that I'm useless at multitasking but I am getting better. There's many a day you'll find me on a conference call whilst loading the washing machine, preparing dinner or updating a webpage. I'm often to be found stood in the playground waiting for my boys to come running, replying to emails on my phone.

The trick is to try and find what I call dead time. These are the moments during each day when you're waiting for something or doing something that doesn't require an awful lot of concentration and then finding a task you can complete or at least start at the same time. Think of all of your quite house hold chores that you can complete whilst on the phone. The person at the other end of the line will never know what you're doing. When you're sitting in the car, waiting for the bank to open, grab your mobile and reply to those emails that you know need answering. Then, think about how you could possibly rearrange your usual schedule. Before starting a business I would spend most of my day cleaning, changing nappies and tidying up after my toddler. I soon realised that if I was going to get any work done, I had to change my routine. I started working during the boys nap times and doing any required cleaning in the evening. This way I was able to use any spare minutes during the peak working hours (9-5) to make any necessary phone calls.

Basically you need to build the same skill set as a top of the league juggler. I'm not going to lie, it is very hard to get used to it at first but very soon, you'll find your stride and before you know it you may even begin juggling with burning clubs!

# Rule Eight: From security to insecurity

In a way I was very fortunate. I had already made the decision to leave work to look after my children so I was never faced with one of the hardest decisions faced by many 'would-be' mumpreneurs. I never had to make the decision to leave a secure, job, with benefits and a regular salary so that I could focus on building my fledgling business. Honestly, looking back, I don't know if I could have done it. I'm constantly speaking to people who have full time jobs whilst trying to start and build a business and they are torn in two. They love their business but at the same time the responsibility to ensure they keep bringing home the bacon means that any chance of giving up employment is slim. The biggest problem they seem to experience is that they are focussing on the low income generated by their part time business and comparing it to the salary that's provided by their job. What many fail to consider is that once they have more time to focus on their growing businesses and more time dedicated to spreading the word and raising the profile of their company their turnover will increase and with that, so will their income.

You need to sit and weigh up the pros and cons of each option without considering the financial aspect. You then need to look at your business plan and see how likely it is that you'll reach the turnover you predicted and when. You need to analyse the figures, the dates and every minute detail before making such a huge life changing decision

# Rule Nine: Routine

When you're nearing the end of your pregnancy, you'll notice everyone telling you just how important a routine is. Once the baby arrives, you quickly realise they were all right. A baby in a good routine provides quality 'me' time for every new mother, without which you may go slightly mad. This rule applies to business too. A routine is vital to ensure that you not only get as much done as possible but it also goes a long way to guaranteeing you get those niggly little admin jobs done on a daily basis.

My day goes a little something like this:

**6am** - Alarm goes off, I get up and desperately fight every natural instinct to crawl back into bed. Sometimes I win, other times I don't.

I take a quick 'wake me up' shower, have a coffee and get started on making myself look human.

**6:45am** - I sit at my laptop and reply to any urgent emails that came in during the night. It's amazing how many people email you in the dead of the night with urgent requests. I don't mind receiving them but the chances of me replying at midnight are slim so I often wonder why people don't just wait until morning.

**7:15am** - I wake my three boys, feed them, wash them and dress them. I run around like a lunatic preparing packed lunches, book bags and inevitably looking for someone's shoe which has mysteriously gone missing. Damn that shoe monster.

**8am** -With the boys pretty much ready I try to spend a little more time at my desk either replying to more emails or adding things to that day's to-do list. I usually manage to squeeze my third cup of coffee in at this point too.

**9:10am** - Having beaten the dreaded school run I am happily back at my lovely desk with a fresh coffee and my list of tasks. I plough into my day knowing that I (more often than not) have five and a half hours of solid work time ahead of me.

**2:45pm** - Back on the school run rolling my eyes as the rain always waits until I'm out of the car and in the playground before it makes an appearance. This way it guarantees that my lovely umbrella is tucked up safe and sound in the boot avoiding doing its job.

**3:45pm** - Back home with my boys, get the dinner on, argue with them until they change out of their uniforms and go through the many letters that have been sent home. Having three children means I get three times the volume of correspondence. I do wonder when they will realise that one of each letter is more than sufficient. Try to reply to urgent emails from my phone whilst sorting the kids, cooking and doing homework.

**7pm** - Get my youngest two to bed and get back to my laptop.

**8pm** - My eldest goes up for the night and I park my behind back at my desk ready for another couple of hours work.

**10/11pm** - Go to bed with my iPad or laptop and a cup of coffee; do a little more work, then fall into a deep, seriously appreciated slumber.

This is my daily routine. This routine keeps me in check and by following it I make the most of my available time. Don't get me wrong, I'm no saint. There are days when all I really want to do is switch on the television, grab a nice cream cake and watch really good, bad TV. Most of the time I manage to resist temptation. Sometimes, I fail.

The fact that many mums start businesses that they can run from a laptop means that there are plenty of ways of sticking to your work routine but you can add a little variety by changing your surroundings. I like to go and work from my parents' house. This way I get to visit them, catch up on family stuff, feel like a good daughter and also keep on top of my business. My new favourite place to work however, has to be Starbucks. I may be a little behind the times but it was only recently that I discovered their free refill policy. Imagine my joy one sunny morning, approaching the counter to order my second filter coffee only to be told that I didn't have to pay!! This may now become my second home. It's easy to be a mobile worker as a mother, even with small children. I used to take my laptop to toddler groups which meant that my 'mummy guilt' was ever so slightly eased as my little ones played with others but I also managed to complete tasks.

Routines are a great way to get through the everyday chores but being a mumpreneur with a routine means you can make it a little more fun!

# Rule Ten: School Holidays Hell

When I worked in sales, we worked to monthly deadlines. As the deadline approached each month, you could feel the tension in the office building by the minute. Every time somebody slammed a telephone receiver down because they simply couldn't make that sale the office atmosphere got a little bit worse. By the time we had reached deadline day nerves were so fraught that people would begin imagining hearing the sound of incoming faxed order. (Yes, we used fax machines. No, it wasn't a hundred years ago. It was a very outdated office).

The feeling that time is running out, there are hundreds of hurdles in your way, and you're never going to hit that deadline is a feeling that you need to get used to during the school holidays and half terms.  You suddenly have so much more to cram into each day. Not only do you have to entertain the little ones, you need to be involved with the entertainment otherwise that old friend 'mummy guilt' kicks in very quickly.   You feel like you are on a constant deadline with the children, with work, with household chores and you will get to a point where all you want to do is curl up into a ball, scream and resume your old life where your business was nothing but a seed of an idea.

Don't feel like a failure. I can guarantee that at least 90% of mothers running a business have felt like that at some point. More often than not during the summer holidays (why oh why are they so long?!?!).

It is going to be an awful lot harder to get things done during these breaks, it's also going to mean working even longer hours than you normally would but in the grand scheme of things it's only for a few weeks every year. The beauty of working for yourself is that you set the rules. You decide when and how your business is going to run. Never lose sight of the fact that you started a business so that you could be more flexible with your children, you could take days off when necessary and you could save money on childcare.

During school breaks, make a point of adding a note to your website. Highlight the fact that order turnaround times may be a little longer than normal or that it may take you a little longer to reply to emails. Customers and clients will only be annoyed if you don't let them know what to expect. If your website states that you will reply to all enquiries within four working hours then they will want a reply within that time frame. If you amend your contact page to state that emails will be replied to within forty-eight hours then you give yourself a little leeway. Also, an added tip, if people are expecting a reply within 2 days but get a reply within 4 hours, they will be much happier with your levels of customer service!

As time goes on, your children will begin to understand that you do have to work for some of each day while they are off school, but while they are still small try to cherish those moments you have them at home. Try to think up games that you can play with your child while you work or even buy a kids desk and create a little home office for them. They will really enjoy 'working' with Mummy!

Don't feel like a bad mother if you use childcare during the school holidays. I usually use a holiday club in the big summer break. This allows me two days each week to focus purely on work and it also gives the children a chance to play with other kids, participate in activities and generally have lots of fun before coming home again to spend time with mummy.

Oh and remember, if people offer to take your little ones for an hour so you can catch up on work.......Say YES! You don't have to pretend to be superwoman all the time.

# Rule Eleven: Inspiring your kids

The lack of enterprise education for children has always frustrated me. A friend of mine took an A-Level in Business Studies and after she told me what was involved, as far as I could see, anything that was relevant seemed like it was put into the curriculum at least fifty years before she took the course.

Over the years, I've asked my eldest son, many times what he wants to be when he's grown up and his answers have changed over and over again. We had all the usual suspects; footballer, doctor, scientist, astronaut and so on but more recently he has started talking about having his own business. Even though he's only eight years old and none of us know what the future has in store for him, it's lovely to know that he's considering all of the options.

For too long when the 'what do you want to be' question has been asked, all children automatically reply with a job rather than a business. Of course there's nothing wrong with that but the world is changing fast and so the way we think has to evolve. As far as I'm concerned, children need to be exposed to the different opportunities available to them from as young an age as possible. They need to be given much more credit when it comes to thinking about their future options.

Don't get me wrong, I'm not saying that my the age of eight they have any idea of the career path they will go on to choose, but I think the younger we provide children with at least an inkling of the options available, the more accepting they are to them.

I love the fact that even though my children know I go home after dropping them off at school each morning, they also know that I'm not lying around, drinking tea and having my brain numbed by trashy TV. Even my youngest, aged four, knows that Mummy comes home and starts work. He's never known things to be any different so he just accepts it as the norm which I adore.

In my opinion, children need to be inspired in as many ways as possible. Whether that's by parents who work full time for other people or parents that work full time and more for themselves. There's nothing more demotivating for our children than for them to see you doing nothing with your life. My children are proud of me and my achievements, even if they don't fully understand what they are or what I do. They know that Mummy doesn't always have time to play and they understand why. They also recognise that hard work, commitment and dedication are vital character traits and that they need to develop theirs to their fullest. I already know, even at such young ages, my children will be budding entrepreneurs. I know this because they're already hustling me! Those boys will go far.

Having your own business not only helps to inspire your children and their futures, it also gives you an identity and gives them a role-model. It helps them realise that you don't always have to conform to the more 'normal' way of life and gives them the basis to investigate their own options when the time comes.

# Rule Twelve: Fear of failure

Many women, especially mothers, never take that leap of faith into the business world because of the fear of failing. This fear can be something that they've created or it could even be down to the seeds of doubt planted by others when the idea is initially mentioned. Either way, it's not a good enough reason not to do it.

In 2009 I started my first business. I had been trawling the web looking for ways to keep my brain active whilst looking after my children and one particular forum caught my eye. It was a forum dedicated to crafters and the more I read the more addicted I became. I would sit up till the wee small hours reading about other people's adventures and successes at craft fairs and various other events. These were women were in the same position as me, at home all day looking after children but they had managed to turn a fun hobby into something that was generating an income. Night after night I would read and digest all of the information being posted online until one day when I realised that I had to be involved. I wanted to join these women and their crafty ways and nobody was going to stop me.

At this stage I should point out that I am not a creative person. Not even a little bit. When I had to make my sons first Easter bonnet I ended up throwing it in a black bag and I borrowed my nephews instead.

I popped into my local craft centre, bought some supplies, came home and started practicing. I'd soon developed my skills and knowledge to the point where I had created something I thought could be sold in shops. Without hesitation I popped to my local card and gift outlet and asked if they'd like to take some on a sale or return basis and they agreed. I was delighted and promptly created an individual stock just for them. Within weeks I'd built a website, created a range of gifts I could sell and started getting online orders. Every email that I received alerting me to the fact that another order had been placed sent my heart racing. The business became very popular very quickly and noticing it's potential my husband built me a workshop to house all of my crafty wares, stock and display pieces for shows.

The highest point for me was when I approached a premier league football team's gift shop and offered to create gifts using their stock so that it was branded with the clubs emblem. They handed me a purchase order there and then and I couldn't have been prouder of myself.

Just under a year into the business I realised the profits just weren't adding up. I'd always ensured that I doubled the cost of the raw materials to reach my RRP but I never accounted for the time it took to create them. When I actually sat down to work out how much I should be charging I knew that there was no way the business could work. The women on those forums were simply doing it to generate a little extra pocket money whereas I wanted to create a successful but more importantly profitable business and I hadn't managed it. I had failed. Even though I knew the facts, it took a while for me to actually close the business down. I'd had a taste of being my own boss and the thought of returning to work made me feel physically sick. I had to think of another idea.

I bet you're wondering why I'm droning on about my failed business. Well, I tried, I failed and I tried again. I knew I had the business sense, I'd just chosen the wrong business for me and now I had to find the right one.

Thankfully after many, many ideas, websites and late night chats with my now business partner, I found my forever business. It took me a few try's, a few tears, many tantrums and lots of sulking but I got there in the end. I can honestly say that if I hadn't been through that experience, I wouldn't be where I am today. Looking back, I'm glad that business failed because it taught me invaluable lessons which still help me every day.

You need to have an 'At least I tried' attitude. I don't know about you but in fifty years I know I'll be much more content knowing I gave it my best shot and didn't just sit thinking about something that never happened.

# Rule Thirteen: Motivation

When you work for yourself, from home, it can be very hard to get motivated every day. Don't tell anyone, but there have been days when I've been known to come in from the school run, kick off my shoes, make a cuppa and sit in front of the TV for a few hours. Not very productive, I know. The worst thing is that even if you feel you deserve this little break, you'll probably find that no matter how hard you try, you just can't enjoy it. No matter how good that episode of Eastenders that you Sky+'d the night before is, there'll be this irritating voice in the back of your head telling you to get up off your backside and get some work done.

That for me is the biggest problem with working from home. I don't have the chance to turn off my computer and leave the office; I'm always in work mode. No matter what time, day or night, I'm constantly running through preparations for meetings or trying to work out how best to word an email. The fact that I work from home also means that if I suddenly realise that I forgot to send an email during the day, I don't need to wait until I arrive at the office the next day to deal with it. Guilt kicks in and I find myself back at my desk sending emails at stupid O'clock.

I have two major motivations. The first is family. I started a business so that I could find that infamous work/life balance and I will continue to work as many hours as I have available until I reach my goals.

My second and possibly bigger motivation is my competition. When I'm not sitting at my desk working, I worry that my competition will manage to push one step ahead, and if that happens because I was too busy watching TV or sleeping, I wouldn't be able to live with myself. This may sound a little obsessive but it works for me and that's the trick. You need to find your trigger. Think about what will be the factors that have you still sitting at your computer at midnight or getting up at 5am to get things done. Those are the things that will get you to your end goal.

Don't get me wrong, we all need a little 'me' time and I always try to schedule that in but if I had to sacrifice it to get ahead.......I would, without question. I suppose, in the back of my mind, I think that I'll have plenty of time to relax late in life when my business has reached its natural peak and I am able to pass responsibilities onto others but until then, the buck stops with me. Every time I get wind of the fact that my competitor has had a particularly good meeting or has managed to secure something great, I make sure I get a better meeting and so on. Every time one of my children asks me for a gift I want to buy them but can't afford to, I work harder and faster than before.

Find your motivation and let it drive you forward.

# Rule Fourteen: No Sick Days

Do you remember when you were a little girl and you woke up with a sore throat? Do you remember your mother putting you back to bed and promising that you could have some ice cream to help soothe the problem? Do you remember how lovely it was to lie back, relax and let your illness pass you by? Try to hold onto those memories, because that's all they will become. Memories.

When you work for yourself, there are no such things as sick days or time off. The really ironic thing is however, that once you become your own boss, you seem to become ill more often! Whether it's simply a case of noticing it more or the stress of trying to fit a thousand things into each day I'll never know but I do know that it's not easy trying to run a business when all you want to do is crawl into bed and let the world disappear for a few hours. Obviously, if you're really, really under the weather then it makes sense to try and relax as much as possible, but it's hard to relax and recover when you know that your to-do list is getting longer by the minute.

You need to think practically and start taking better care of yourself. I know that time becomes limited in the SEW (Self Employment World), but making a little time for yourself each day will pay you back tenfold.  Little things like taking vitamin supplements, especially during the winter will help steer any potential colds away. A relaxing bubble bath in the evening will help you to unwind and also sleep better meaning that you should wake up fully refreshed each morning and ready to face another day.

The reality of the situation is that you will rarely become so ill that you're unable to carry out even the basic day to day duties but you should always have somebody on standby just in case you are bedridden by a sudden and unexpected case of mumpreneuritis.

# Rule Fifteen: Childcare costs

The cost of childcare is ridiculous, fact! To give you an idea just how high it is I'll share with you the costs I used to incur.

When I originally returned to work following the birth of my first son I was lucky enough to have a boss who agreed to flexible working hours. I would work from Home on a Monday and Friday and in the office the other three days. My child minding costs for an average of 12 days per month were £400. I was perfectly happy with this figure but if I'd continued to work after my second and third sons were born the costs would have been ridiculous, and they wonder why so many single parents end up on benefits?!

To be honest, had I returned to work after each one of my boys and had to pay childcare coupled with the usual household outgoings it would have meant that by the end of the month I would have broken even or, sometimes, even made a loss. It just wasn't worth it.

More and more women are realising how expensive, good childcare is and it's not the sort of thing you can scrimp on. With this realisation more and more mums are looking into their options and beginning businesses.

Don't be fooled into thinking that self-employment means you never have to pay for childcare again. When your children are small you will need a day every now and again when you have to focus on your business and your business alone. If you have friends and family that are supportive and they're willing to help out with childcare, don't be too proud to take them up on their offers. As your children get bigger and start school, you will have a minimum of five hours to work each day but by this time your business may have grown to the point that it needs more than five hours and external childcare may be your best option.

My sister once told me that as soon as children start schools you day becomes shorter. Needless to say I thought she was losing the plot. Five whole hours to do nothing but work with no interruptions, how could my day become shorter? Imagine my surprise when I found out she was right. Obviously I'm not talking about the Sandman rearranging the clocks or making hours shorter but once your children reach school age and you finally have a little independence, it really does feel like the days have halved. You spend the first half of the day working and the second half dealing with children, housework, cooking, homework, laundry and bedtimes. All of a sudden it's 11pm and you wonder who ran off with your day.

If you have access to and can afford quality childcare then use it where possible. I have an arrangement with the out of school club to take my boys when I have meetings in the big smoke. This way I'm not panicking to get home in time to collect them and they get to spend time playing with their friends. Win, win.

After thinking about the costs I incurred for childcare I did a little investigating and discovered that the average family pays xxxx per year for childcare. It's an astronomical outgoing for any family, no wonder more and more mothers are joining the mumpreneur revolution!

# Rule Sixteen: Social Media

For me, the biggest drawback when it comes to working from home is the loneliness. Don't get me wrong, my inbox has new deliveries every few minutes and my phone is quite often hot due to excessive use but in the beginning I craved adult company. My husband was working full time and so were all of my friends I had very few people to call for a chat in the middle of the day and I felt isolated.

Facebook became my most visited website. I picked it up fairly quickly and found it a great way to pass time and interact with my friends whilst they were at work. Once I'd started my business I realised that Facebook also had its business advantages and was a great marketing tool, but it wasn't until I discovered Twitter that my thirst for company was well and truly quenched. For me and thousands of others, Twitter isn't just a way to interact with customers and display great customer service skills, it's also a place to rally support, network with others in the same position as you and believe it or not, form some amazing friendships. Some of my biggest supporters, mentors and inspirations are people I've never actually met. They are people I've connected with, chatted with and bonded with over social networking.

If you intend to be a work at home mother you NEED to register an account on Twitter first and foremost. I'll be totally honest and say it's not that easy to get into. It took me a few weeks of dedicated tweeting, and playing around with settings and platforms before I really got involved but I don't know where I'd be without it now. Twitter is a lifeline to the outside world and because you're hiding behind a screen, it gives you the confidence to approach people you might not otherwise have met.

Don't ever underestimate the power of social networking sites such as Facebook, Twitter and even Linkedin. They are becoming the most powerful FREE marketing tools available to business owners and give you the opportunity to get your brand in front of hundreds, thousands and possibly millions of potential customers.

More importantly, during those wee small hours when you're still replying to emails or composing proposals, it can be your lifeline to the outside world. After all, you won't be the only mumpreneur still working online at that time of night, there are hundreds of users just waiting for your tweet.

# Rule Seventeen: No money

As with any new business owner, you have to be prepared to not only work excessive hours, but to work excessive hours and not earn anything. If you're lucky, you're business will cost nothing to start and will begin generating an income fairly quickly, however, this is unlikely. Most businesses need money to get going and take a while to start repaying their start-up debt. You need to have a plan in place to ensure you can get by with a minimal income.

My first business generated a sporadic but good income but I never quite priced my products enough to cover labour and ended up breaking even for a lot of work. My current business began generating a regular income almost immediately and I firmly believe that it's because I planned more accurately. I now sell a service rather than a product which instantly means I have I higher profit margin. My business takes very little time to run now that it's beginning to establish itself in the market place and there are no real costs involved. I currently run at a 92% profit margin compared to a zero profit margin with my retail business. I'm not trying to imply that you'll earn more by selling a service as this simply isn't the case but if you're selling a product, it may take a little longer to break even and generate profits.

Personally, I found that the easiest way to manage financially in the beginning was to try and be a little smarter with my spending. I worked out every which way I could reduce my outgoings and then signed up to websites like Moneysavingexpert.com as their community boards are full of great offer and tips on ways to save a small fortune every day.

In those early days, I found it very useful to focus on saving money rather than making money. Maybe I was wrong but it worked for me and I know others have found this way of thinking helped them too.

# Rule Eighteen: Ditch those joggers

We all know what school runs are like and there are very few mums who enjoy partaking in this activity. It's so easy to just run a flannel over your face, pull on the first clean and un-creased clothes you can find and shove a hat on, after all, you're only going to be hanging around a playground and then going back to the safety of your home. The problem with this is that wearing a pair of joggers and your oldest cardigan, albeit your most comfortable cardigan doesn't exactly get you into the working frame of mind.

Every morning, I have a shower, do my hair and make-up and get dressed for a day in the office. I may not be going into an actual office but I've noticed that this really does help to get me in the right frame of mind.  Research shows that when companies have a 'casual' day and employees wear jeans etc. for the office, the productivity levels reduce significantly. It's the same in schools. Children are more focused and work more efficiently when they are in uniform as opposed to on 'own clothes days'.

Whether you plan to work from home, Starbucks or even a park bench, dress to impress and I promise you it will make a difference to your work.

# Rule Nineteen: The commute

Personally, I really miss the commute to work. In all fairness my commute took about fifteen minutes and I rarely hit any traffic but I do miss it. That fifteen minutes in the car on the way to the office gave me the time to switch from mummy mode to work mode. When I got to work I was no longer a mum a wife or a cleaner, I was just me. Hard worker and appreciated employee.

The only way I have managed to get that feeling back is by taking a different route home from the school run in the mornings. It's not quite the same but it really does help. When I leave the house in the morning I am a mummy taking my children to school but when I leave the playground I am a business woman on my way to work. Using a slightly different route does help me to split those two personalities apart. It works so well that I've now started leaving the house for a five minute drive even when the children are off school. Even as I write this I know it makes me sound slightly deranged but sometimes it can be very hard to transform from one person to the other.

It may work for you or it may not, but it's worth a try. Anything that gets you motivated and makes you more productive is worth a go surely!?

# Rule Twenty: Attitude

As cheesy as it sounds your attitude goes a long way towards the success of your business. If you sit at your computer or make phone calls thinking that everyone is going to turn you down then chances are everyone IS going to turn you down.

There are a few little tricks to help to get you into a positive, working frame of mind:

- Every morning, give yourself a little pep talk. You don't have to be in front of a mirror or even in a quiet room; you can do it in your head where no-one can interrupt. If you do have the chance to say the words aloud then do it. Even if you think you sound silly, who's going to hear?
- Print some motivational quotes and stick them on your wall. If you don't want them to be displayed for all of your visitors to see, stick them on the inside of your cupboard door.
- Create a vision board and take a look at it every morning. A vision board is a type of poster designed by you to display images representing your long term goals. Whenever you wake up on the wrong side of the bed, a quick glance at it should give you a good kick up the behind.

# Rule Twenty one: Childcare

The most attractive benefit of self-employment for any mother is the flexibility. Once children reach the age of four they enter into the schooling system and if you have a full time job this opens up a whole new world of worries. In any given school year, children have approximately ........days of holidays and the average employer will credit each member of staff with around 20 days of paid holiday leave. Now, I'm not necessarily great with the numbers but even I can see a gap the size of the Grand Canyon there.

There are many options available to working parents when it comes to childcare, but each comes with a fairly hefty price tag, especially if you have more than one child that needs looking after. Whilst having your own business does mean working long, unsocial and difficult hours it also gives you the opportunity to be more flexible when it comes to out of school arrangements. You can choose whether to send the children to play schemes, school holiday clubs or simply cut your hours down so that you only work in the evenings. Whatever decision you make you can be safe in the knowledge that if you were employed, your decision would be based on your employers' flexibility rather than your own and your children's needs.

You may be reading this thinking this is the answer to all your prayers, but, as with everything in life, there is a flip-side. For me, family holidays are no longer dreamt about or looked forward to. Each time we book a holiday, a feeling of anxiety begins deep in the pit of my stomach. With every passing day that feeling grows and grows until, yet again, I'm nearing breaking point. Why? Because I am the heart and soul of my business, with me gone, my business is gone. I control and do everything and in those early stages you'll more than likely find that you're in the same position.

To be able to truly relax, you need to be able to take a step back and unfortunately, young businesses can't always afford to pay outside staff, therefore you're not only left holding the baby but you're also left holding the business. If you have children of school age when you start your business it's well worth sitting down and thinking about how you will run your business during those long summer holidays. It's almost two months of being full time parents, so trying to keep up with your to-do list won't be easy. Try to implement plans and systems that will automate some of your daily tasks. For each job you can do this with, you could be saving yourself up to an hour each day which you can then spend with your children.

As time goes on, try to bring somebody into the business that you trust to take on a little responsibility at a time. I'm not necessarily talking about a full time or even part time employee but maybe a virtual assistant or admin angel that you can teach about how your business works.

In theory, within a year or two, you should be able to leave your business for a few hours, days or even a week to take (what will without doubt be) a much needed break. Those school summer holidays are long enough for kids so trying to squeeze in a few days away can make all the difference to them and to you. They get a break outside of the house and you get a break outside of your business.

Hopefully, after a few days away, you'll all return, refreshed and ready to take on the world!

# Rule Twenty-two: Visiting hours are over

If you were employed and working in an office block would your family and friends pop in throughout the day to say hi and grab a cuppa with you? Would they give you a call you at various point during the day for a quick gossip? No. Yet when you work from home they all seem to think it's perfectly normal to call round, grab a brew, take a seat on your sofa and start chatting. They aren't doing it on purpose, they just don't seem to realise that during the day, your home is your place of work and by visiting you they are eating into your precious working time and after all, time is money. Did I really just say that?!

Try to explain to people that during certain hours you will be busy working and it's not practical for them to call on you. If they support your business they won't have a problem and they will totally understand. If they complain or start making snide comments about your 'business' then you know that they were never fully supporting you anyway. Make sure that all of your work calls come through to your mobile phone. That way you turn your landline onto silent or just ignore it when it rings. As time goes on, people will begin to realise that actually you are serious about your business and that it's simply not a hobby. They will begin to respect your working hours and understand that there are barriers that they shouldn't cross.

If you make the rules clear from the start then you should be able to avoid upsetting anyone and getting involved in any unnecessary arguments.

# Mummy Guilt

For me and the thousands of other mumpreneurs out there, the biggest downside to being self-employed has to be mummy guilt.

Whether you have a business or not, as a mother, the feeling of guilt is always right there, ready and waiting to pounce. Maybe because you feel you haven't spent enough quality time with your children, maybe you feel that the meals you provide them aren't nutritious enough, or maybe you simply forgot to go and see them in a school play. Whatever the reason, mummy guilt becomes a permanent fixture in the life of every single mother.....unless of course, you're Mary Poppins.

Once you start a business the mummy guilt seems to show up on a much more regular basis. I seem to constantly be saying 'just give me a minute, let me just finish this email, mummy will come and play just as soon as I've finished this job'. It's as if I have this constant string of phrases that basically translate as 'go away for five minutes whilst I attend to this urgent job'. Even as I write this I'm feeling guilty because my boys are in the other room playing games whilst I sit with my laptop yet again.

My children are beginning to understand that I do have things that need to be done and that I can't spend all day playing Hungry Hippos or hide and seek but that doesn't stop me from feeling like the worst mother in the world. I try to allocate a certain amount of time each day to spending time with my children, even if it's a case of me sitting alongside them on the sofa with my laptop whilst they watch a movie. They know I'm not really watching, but they really do appreciate the fact that I'm spending time with them.

It's so easy to get caught up in the running of your business and the excitement that goes along with that, but you can find little ways of spending quality time with your children so that they don't feel second best to your business.

Make sure that even if you don't eat at the same time as your kids that you sit with them whilst they have their dinner. Use this time to chat to them about their day at school, the friends they played with and the work they did. If your children are below school age then take a little extra time to play games, have cuddles and generally have some fun. There are very few emails that are so urgent that they require an immediate reply. An email or a phone call can usually wait, your children can't.

Try to remember that you started your business so that you could find that family/life balance that you hear others talking about so happily and that your children are young for only a short time. Take the time to enjoy your children while you can, spend time with them, play with them and love them, before you know it, they'll have grown up and left home.

# Conclusion

Absolutely! There is no greater feeling than knowing you are not only raising your children but your also building something that will benefit you and your family in the years to come. The satisfaction that comes from watching something you created grow from an idea to reality is second to none but to be able to do that and also continue being involved in the day to day upbringing of your children is an amazing experience.

As you've probably gathered from reading this book, it's not the easy option. There is no such thing as an instant success. Whatever idea you choose to expand upon you will have to put in days, weeks, months and even years of hard work to make it come to fruition. It will be tiring and there will be times when throwing the towel in will seem like the answer to all of your problems but you just need to keep going. If you were to draw up a list of pros and cons of starting a business, and you were totally honest when compiling the list, initially the cons would more than likely outweigh the pros but you have to ignore the downsides and focus on the positives.

I've made it abundantly clear that self-employment is not the easy route for anyone let alone a full time mother but no matter how any people who ask my advice, I always answer with the same thing…….

**JUST DO IT!**

# Case Studies

**Vivien Sable**
www.viviensable.com

I suppose as a Psychotherapist you may think I have all the tools to survive on my journey? In part I would say I have, but in order to survive I have recruited the support of my own Psychotherapist, a Clinical Supervisor, occasional Acupuncturist, fabulous hairdresser (who happens to be my husband) and some amazing friends and supporters. I also try to take care of my own health needs too. I'm a bit of a Zumba queen and I enjoy five visits per week to various keep fit type classes. I've just begun on my Karate journey too so watch out. Are you keeping up here? I appreciate I seem to be a busy working Mama.

My journey into Psychotherapy is one thing, and navigating the mothering and clinical role has taken time to master but in addition to the above I embarked upon writing a book. It is my journey into securing a publishing deal for my baby book that has been incredible. Pursuing this dream and only ever believing I could do it is what I want to share with you.

Some seven years ago, following the birth of my daughter Blossom I made some astounding discoveries into the 'world of baby'. After completing my clinical studies in 2010 I decided I would simply knuckle-down and write a book about it. If I'm honest, I think my family and friends thought I must have been losing my mind! I'd only just finished my most recent degree and there I was starting on another journey, but once I get a bee in my bonnet there is no stopping me! I then decided I would simply write it. I gave up a lucrative psychotherapy contract, shuffled around my clinics, and worked seventeen hours a day for three to four months. I shared the content of my manuscript with a few close friends and clinicians who seemed to be astounded by both the content and the journey. After working away for three to four months I had, to my amazement completed 40,000 words.

In the meantime I had started to build my LinkedIn profile, I had a website and blog built and I did as much as I could in terms of networking. I then carefully selected people to globally network with who were (and still are) involved in parenting, writing books, baby experts, psychologists, and PR and publishing executives. Once I'd finished my manuscript I cold-called twenty LinkedIn contacts and asked them if they would be willing to review my manuscript. To my astonishment they all agreed, and I gained permission from all of my reviewers to use their comments. One of the reviewers was particularly helpful. She suggested I edit the manuscript and even more astonishing once I had, she asked me if she could take it to a publishing house in Australia! After a few months (Publishing is a long process) the publishing house sent me an amazing email. The said, they would not be accepting my manuscript as my book was going to sell millions of copies all over the world. They said I needed to approach a massive publishing house like Random House who had large-scale distribution & marketing divisions. I secured a publishing deal with Random House, and well, the rest is history!

The point of sharing this with you is to say you can survive, be a mumpreneur and you can keep following your dream. Here below are my hints to surviving and succeeding:

- Write about or work in an area you are passionate about
- Speak from the heart and the words will jump straight from your heart on to the pages and into the boardroom.
- Stay focused on the subject
- Never give up
- Be creative
- Visualise your dream and make it your reality
- Share your passion with likeminded people – they may wish to support you

- Take care to juggle carefully your work/home life and try to do things as a family – I recommend Karate!

# Case Studies

**Zoe**

www.BabyDubois.co.uk

I started my business after I had my daughter, mainly as a source of income but also to fulfil a long held ambition to be my own boss. Armed with a couple of books on marketing, I started off making a range of baby bibs and slings in unusual and colourful fabrics and booked a slot at a local craft show. I had precious little idea how many I was going to sell but I decided that the best I could hope for would be all of them! Every moment I had free, I would be pattern cutting, sewing, or fixing on poppers until I was pretty much on my knees. As a single parent I was pinning a lot on this venture which spurred me on even when I was falling asleep at the machine. The first craft show was a real eye opener. I made a few sales (not quite everything!) but it gave me a great chance to network with other stall holders and chat to the punters. I spent a lot of time looking at other stands, taking notes about how they lit them and arranged their stock. I also used the opportunity to try out some pricing models to see what worked. I took the ideas onto the next show and started to build an online business alongside the craft shows. It was a great start and a confidence boost that I could do it and I've gone from strength to strength since then. I'm still knackered but I'm confident that going into business will help me keep my self-respect and help provide for my daughter and I.

# Case Studies

## Julia Suzuki
www.juliasuzuki.com

How do I juggle being an author of a highly accredited children's series, a property consultant and a beauty and fashion expert? Wow if I had a thousand bucks every time that question was asked. 'How do you do it?' 'Do you get any time for yourself?' and I reply always with the same phrase, my time is for myself, I love what I do, every bit of it, its all me. I just add my career to the list of Mother, Cleaner, Shopper, Car Maintainer, Accountant, Beautician, Administrator and every other task in my day and well, what's another four of five hats when you have thirty. And I love hats, each one allows you to express yourself in a different way, and adds to the beauty of life's exquisiteness.

The answer to how? is discipline. An organizational structure given to me by a famous business coach Brian Tracy of prioritizing in 15-minute slots. This is after two sheets one of listing, and then one of prioritising. With this approach you really can get six times more done in any day. Its genius and ticking off the list is so gratifying that it gives you somewhat of a healthy addiction. I learned too from my business mentorship with David Lloyd the gym legend, who built up a gym business that he floated on the stock market for 200 million pounds. He once told me how he drove around each of the eight London sites in one Christmas Eve. His attitude of hard work combined with terrier like determination rubbed off and you get so adept at taking action all the time that you can still do it with a smile on your face while feeling the inner power inside. Not forgetting 'Universal' intervention, you just keep going and somehow you make it.

I also keep things simple, (huge time saving, simplicity). Simple food takes less time, wearing dresses takes less time to coordinate than two piece outfits, grabbing fruit is my saviour and if I arrive to the gym unglamourised so what, it shows I mean business.

My organisation skills took some necessary adjustment. One day I was so hurried that i missed a time check, so I threw my coat on over my nightie to do a school run with my son.. How many other Mums have done this and wont admit it? Poll please!. I laughed all the way there, and it felt somewhat of a magical experience, like some secret sin. Now every time I see a Mum in a tightly buttoned coat I get this urge to want to check if they are secret sinners too.

When people say I cant, I no longer say I can, I moved up from that one. I now say 'I am'

# Case Studies

**Abi Purser**
www.longcroftcathotel.co.uk

36 year old Abi Purser opened her first luxury cat hotel in Welwyn Garden City in 2010. When she couldn't find a cattery up to the standard she wanted for 21 year old Norman, their much loved ginger and white tomcat. Also, Abi had resigned from a full time job running a saddlery, where she'd worked for 12 years, after she gave birth to son Harry in 2007.

Longcroft Cat Hotel is run by Abi, in the garden of her home, with help from husband Matt on the website, and their three children, Millie, 17, Harry 4 and Freddie, 2. They turned their vegetable patch, which Abi says they weren't very good at keeping anyway, into six luxury, custom built suites, to look after their feline guests.

As you would expect at any 5 star hotel, everything from the wrought iron designer cat beds with soft pillows and individually decorated bedroom suites to gourmet menus served on bone china, has been designed around the feline guest's wellbeing and their owner's peace of mind.

It has been such a runaway success that the business is now being offered as a franchise to other cat loving would be entrepreneurs. Abi says" We literally spotted a gap in a market that nobody knew existed. Instead of trying to ascertain how to make catteries 'better' we invented a cat hotel and then worked out what that would look like and how to turn it into a business."

Instead of starting a business and then adjusting their lifestyle around it, Abi and Matt created the perfect business for their lifestyle.

The Longcroft Cat Hotel has had praise and testimonials from hundreds of cat owners who have been able to go on holiday, or in a time of crisis, have been able to leave their cats with Abi, knowing that their much loved pets will have the same amount, if not more,

Love and attention that they get at home. The fact that Longcroft enjoys bookings months in advance, is testament to the dedication and truly premium service offered.

Some owners will never send their cats anywhere but Longcroft ever again. One cat called Gizmo, had meowed the place down in every other cattery he stayed at and his owners said he always came home with a sore throat. The jazz and classical music played in his suite at Longcroft made him so content there was no more caterwauling from Gizmo when he was away from home. Then there are some cats who have some some issues - like Diesel, who arrived with a carriage clock that chimed on the hour - she was so shy that she hid under her pillow on the first night, but after lots of cuddles and one-to-one attention, she was as happy as could be and walking around with the other guests. Florinha, who was rescued by her owners when they were on holiday in Spain, had to have King Prawns at 4.30pm every day and Cookie, the Tortoiseshell, only drinks from a pint glass!

Abi says: "Running a business from home and looking after cats is my dream job. When we first set up the business, we knew that there was a demand for a truly 5 star cattery dedicated to looking after much loved feline guests. We just massively underestimated the level of that demand.

# Case Studies

**Cara Sayer**
www.snoozeshade.com

That light-bulb moment - when you come up with an idea, remember that, if it's something you need, then there are probably hundreds and thousands of others who need it too. One thing I've learned is that if you're passionate about your idea and you believe in it, others will believe in it too. There are lots of sunshades but none that are specifically designed to help babies sleep when out and about during naptime. I kept complaining to friends about the fact that I couldn't find something to use instead of the things I draped over my daughter's pram to help her sleep and everyone kept saying 'why don't you come up with something yourself?'.

Do your homework - once you think you've spotted a gap in the market, do your research and don't be afraid to ask as many people as possible what they think of your idea. Ask your family and friends and anyone else who might be in the market for your product or service. I took a prototype everywhere with me in case I came across someone who was willing to tell me what they thought. It wasn't always favourable but mostly people couldn't believe that something like SnoozeShade didn't already exist.

Spotting an opportunity - at that critical point where I was going to have to bite the bullet and decide to go ahead or not, my mother persuaded me to exhibit at a trade show in London to see what the nursery industry thought of my idea. With only one hand-stitched prototype to show and some packaging we'd put together ourselves, we were able to gather lots of invaluable feedback from the very people who would be stocking the product if we went ahead with it - and it was at the show that we took our first order for 100 units which was incredibly exciting.

Think big - right from the start, it's a good idea to try to develop a brand rather than just a single product. This is what I've done with SnoozeShade and I've established a strong market presence and brand identity using a variety of methods - social media (Twitter, Facebook, etc.,) is great for generating interest in and demand for your products, as are blogs, and you can spread the word through radio and TV appearances, special offers and competitions, and exhibiting at international trade and consumer shows.

Don't feel guilty - as a parent, you'll probably feel guilty about the amount of time you have to devote to your business at the expense of your family. I still worry about not spending enough time with my daughter but child-minders, flexible after-school care facilities and day camps during the school holidays are invaluable for freeing up those extra hours and keeping on top of it all.

# Case Studies

**Louise Guinda**
www.safedreams.co.uk

I came up with the idea of a breathable alternative to cot bumpers after a horrible experience that took place when my son was a new-born baby. Like most babies, he loved to snuggle into anything soft in his cot, and one day I found him with his face completely submerged into his cot bumper, blue in the face and really struggling to breathe. I was horrified and stopped using the bumper but then he began to get his arms trapped between the bars and lose his dummy through the gaps on a nightly basis.

I discovered that many other parents were having the same problem but surprisingly there was no solution available at the time in the UK. This was my 'light bulb' moment; inspired by the breathable mesh bumpers that I had seen in the US, I wanted to make a prettier, softer version with a 100% cotton inner surface.

As I had no experience of manufacturing and selling a product, it took me 2 years to launch the Cot Wrap. Looking back, I could have launched the product much sooner if I had had more confidence in myself and also if I hadn't been afraid to ask for advice from others. I would strongly recommend that mums who are looking to start a business get out and meet other successful Mumpreneurs. Most of us are happy to help and quite flattered to be asked for advice.

I am now lucky enough to be able to afford to put my son in nursery four days a week but back when I started the business a few years ago he was at home all day with me and I had to take advantage of every quiet moment. I have many ambitions which involve travelling but unfortunately they have to be put on hold until my son is much older. Not that I'm complaining, I love being with him as much as possible.

My top tips are to believe in yourself and don't always assume that others know best. Also, take advantage of all of the help offered to you and don't feel guilty about working to build a good future for your children. Finally, get a cleaner! It will give you an extra 3 hours a week which will offset the cost and an incentive to keep the house tidy which improves your productivity I find (personally I cannot work in a messy house!).

# Case Studies

### Danny Maddocks (dadpreneur)
www.babysfirstcalendar.co.uk

Starting a business is like having a new-born baby. You wish and plan and prepare for months and sometimes years and when you finally have it and all your dreams come true reality kicks in and the real work begins.

You can never switch off, you constantly worry about it, you wonder if you are doing the best by it and it can seem like forever before it stops with the "take, take, and take" and finally gives something back.

Having a baby is hard. Starting a business is hard.

So why would anyone in their right mind do either? Because the rewards are amazing! Not just in monetary terms either, plenty of people start their own small businesses earning less in the early years than they could in full time employment. Fact. Yet owning your own business gives you a real sense of achievement, a feeling of wellbeing, more free time to spend as you choose and can lead to a whole world of opportunities that you never thought possible (I didn't expect to be chatting with BBC Dragons Den star Theo Paphitis at the IoD - but it happened!).

If you are thinking of starting your own business the single most important thing you have to do is take action. Thousands of people have thousands of amazing business ideas every single day yet they never do anything about it, you may heard them at some point say "I had that idea 10 years ago"? Maybe they did, but an idea alone is worthless if you do not take the action needed to bring that idea to life.

Look at successful people in any industry wherever they may be and how ever you define their success and you will find one common factor for sure – they all took action. They took the steps necessary to become a success. And you should too.

There is a wealth of really useful (and free) information on the internet to help you start your own business, you should start taking action right now (once you finish this book of course!).

# Case Studies

## Rebekah Harriman
www.rrva.co.uk

Staying positive and tuning out the naysayers

Staying positive about running your own business can be very hard at times. Especially at those times that everyone who sets up a business has, when you have no clients, no money coming in and you are terrified of how you are going to pay the next bill or go food shopping. If you don't panic and are honest with yourself these times pass quickly and you can spot them better, and take action to prevent them.

When I first started out being self employed, all of 3 years ago, I had many, many of those moments of wondering what I had got myself into. Worried and rather panic stricken about how I was going to pay my mortgage that month I ended up working with people I shouldn't have done just for the money; people who simply didn't pay me or were not in my identified niche or my gut was screaming at me to walk away from. These were not good decisions and did not help me meet the bills in the long run, left me very stressed out and with a business that really wasn't going anywhere, let alone where I wanted it to. These initial moments were, however, often caused by a helpful friend or relatives comment, advice or concerned enquiry as to how things were going financially. Helpful suggestions about it maybe being best to get a proper job so I had a regular income and not to forget I had children to clothe and feed abounded. What I have learned to do is recognize who these people are in my life and carefully avoid talking about my business with them and tuning out the things they say about it. With the rest of my life they are fine, supportive family and friend just not when it comes to running a business! It is ok to do this too, no guilt involved. I have just copied my children's tactic of not listening to those people who aren't really that supportive of what I am trying to achieve. That doesn't mean that you should ignore all criticism, not at all, you can learn from constructive criticism and build a better business and the people who give it usually don't leave you in a blind panic and spiral of worry about what you are dong! You need to seek out both online and offline other like-minded people who you can ask questions of, who inspire you and make you want to achieve more. I personally go to the Mumpreneur Conference every year; I call it my yearly injection of self-belief. I couldn't keep growing and envisioning greater things without that self-belief and confidence in my services. I still have those panic stricken moments and they are still usually caused by some casual remark by someone close to me but I have strategies in place to handle them better and not let them get to me as much, and a group of people who will always tell me that they believe in me even my belief has wobbled.

# Case Studies

### Ciara Clifford BabyTrivia

See the 3 best things about being a mumpreneur as:

- Doing what you love doing
- Being able to find balance between work and home
- hinking to yourself - I can't believe I have achieved this!

The 3 worst things are:

- Never switching off
- Not receiving a salary every month
- The worry...what if this fails....

### Tima Reshad Coco Nailbar

Bad:
- Barely have time for me
- Always feel guilty I'm not doing enough or working hard enough
- Always tired

Good:
- As the baby gets older, it gets easier
- Once the baby goes to school, I have work ready and waiting for me
- I have the enjoyment of a beautiful baby and a flourishing business simultaneously!

# Case Studies

**Natalie Trice www.tallypr.co.uk**

- Best 3 things about being a mumpreneur
- You are your own boss and can decide who you do and don't' work with
- You get a huge amount of pride from working for yourself and when you do well, you know it was all you!
- You get to go to school plays, open days, sports days, be around to dish out love when the boys are poorly and go for a Starbucks because you are worth it!
- Worse 3 things about being a mumpreneur
- YOU have to motivate yourself everyday - if you don't do it no one else will!
- You have to work even when you are sick and in bed - if you don't, no one else will!
- You have to do everything from lick the stamps and make the tea to writing business plans and pitch for business - if you don't do it no one else will!

# Case Studies

**Kez Luckett**
www.mummysmaid.co.uk

Worse 3 things about being a mumpreneur

- Knowing when to stop!!! As there are never enough hours in the day, and I think as mums we constantly try to squeeze in just a little bit more, whether it's that hour before the children wake up or the 4 hours after they have gone to sleep
- The constant juggling act between phone calls, paperwork, and children
- The unknown! Unfortunately when you set up a new business you don't know, what you don't know and it's a steep learning curve. Best piece of advice is to take every day at a time.
- Best 3 things about being a mumpreneur
- Running my own business, it's my baby, almost like having a third child
- Flexibility- to be able to attend the school plays and music productions.
- Being in a business that helps so many other mums.

# Case Studies

### Cheryl White
www.enhancemychance.com

Best:

- Not having to leave your child(ren) with someone else to earn money
- Keeping your mind active and not going a little craz
- Setting a good example to your child(ren), that having children doesn't mean you have to give up your dreams and you can still be a success.

Worst:

- Poorly baby = no work done
- You are always at work
- BEING TIRED.

### Rachel Norrington
www.treehousejewellery.co.uk

- **The 3 Best are** - getting to be a stay at home mom and still have a career, being able to attend sport's day, nativity etc. , making your own decisions

- **The 3 Worst are** - Trying to juggle looking after 3 little children and be effective for the business, not being able to leave your work behind at the end of the day, making your own decisions.

# Case Studies

**Wendy Powell**
www.mutusystem.com

Worse 3 things:

- Working till midnight every night to then overhear your 6 year old tell someone 'my Mummy doesn't have a job'
- 2 small children with a sandwich in one hand & a drink in the other clambering over you when you're at the laptop
- Telling your children they can't play games or watch TV when you're permanently glued to your iPhone

Best 3 things:

- As I do the school run in workout gear ' Mummy you've got your work clothes on'
- Knowing my kids are growing up seeing their mummy work & run a business, but also seeing their mummy
- Spending the day on the beach with my kids playing & my husband filming me exercise, is actually WORK

# Just Do it:
# Rules to go from the School Run to the Boardroom

Published by
**Negotiis Books**

**Laura Rigney**

www.ingramcontent.com/pod-product-compliance
Lightning Source LLC
Chambersburg PA
CBHW021021180526
45163CB00005B/2058